Praise for The Instant Anxiety Solution

"*The Instant Anxiety Solution* is full of practical advice and simple hacks on how to reduce your anxiety level. Readers will undoubtedly gain some helpful insights and ideas to help them (and their loved ones) improve and attain personal physical, mental and emotional health goals. A must-read for anybody wrestling with anxiety."

–Beth Hedva, PhD, author of *Betrayal, Trust and Forgiveness*

"*The Instant Anxiety Solution* is a must-read for anyone suffering from anxiety. I will most definitely be sharing these strategies with my Hollywood clients. I particularly like Michelle's holistic approach. I am a true believer that we must deal with the individual as a whole on our path to wellness."

–Ramona Braganza, celebrity fitness trainer

"*The Instant Anxiety Solution* is an essential read for anyone suffering from anxiety. Michelle has a true passion and skill for her trade of helping people lead healthier lives. Finding a veteran coach as well as a talented health and fitness expert is rare. I particularly admire Michelle's multi-disciplinary approach to health."

–Michelle Lovitt, MSc, fitness trainer and author of *Exercise for Your Muscle Type*

THE

INSTANT
ANXIETY
SOLUTION

THE
INSTANT
ANXIETY
SOLUTION

5 Simple Steps
to Quiet Your Mind
& Achieve Calm

MICHELLE BITON
Foreword by
Nadine Macaluso, Ph.D.

Hatherleigh Press is committed to preserving
and protecting the natural resources of the earth.
Environmentally responsible and sustainable practices are
embraced within the company's mission statement.

Visit us at www.hatherleighpress.com.

THE INSTANT ANXIETY SOLUTION

Text Copyright © 2024 Michelle Biton

Library of Congress Cataloging-in-Publication
Data is available.

ISBN: 978-1-57826-982-2

Author Photo by Tamara Leigh Photography

Cover and Interior Design by Carolyn Kasper

Printed in the United States

10 9 8 7 6 5 4 3 2 1

CONTENTS

FOREWORD

NADINE MACALUSO, PH.D.

Everyone experiences feelings of anxiety and stress. Maybe you're fighting with a friend or preparing for a big interview; or perhaps you're worried about your children, your finances, or the current state of the world in general.

Anxiety is the feeling of helplessness or anticipatory fear. If we're being honest with ourselves, we've each felt this way at one point or another. It is a natural part of life and a regular part of the human experience. But when anxious feelings involve excessive worry, fear, and stress, and your capacity to cope is overwhelmed, anxiety can get in the way of your well-being. Anxiety disorders exist on a spectrum—they can interrupt your day-to-day life in small but noticeable ways or be debilitating in severe cases. The good news is that there is hope no matter where you fall on this spectrum.

With the soaring cost of quality mental health care, finding the help you need can be difficult. Yet, as I tell every one of my clients, you are your own best healer. There are countless resources to aid your recovery—*The Instant Anxiety Solution* is undoubtedly a book we all need to read. It is like having an anxiety coach in your pocket because Michelle offers valuable information and easy self-help techniques to support you in alleviating your anxiety symptoms. She provides tips in small, easily digestible portions, which allow you to feel more confident and in control—the opposite of helplessness.

Our world has evolved, and so has our knowledge of evidence-based practices to treat anxiety. All signs point to a holistic approach that employs both the mind and the body; the two are inseparable for achieving well-being. As a somatic psychotherapist, I particularly enjoy the holistic approach that Michelle suggests for managing anxiety. If your mind's racing thoughts fuel your anxiety, this book has practical tools to help you control those thoughts. If the fear in your body manifests with a racing heart, shortness of breath, or shaky hands, this book will be the answer to soothing your stress. Blending her expertise in holistic nutrition with psychology and neuroscience, Michelle brings forth a unique perspective and offers skills that have the power to help you reach your potential.

In these pages, you'll learn to overcome anxiety by recognizing it, naming it, and applying a specific technique to relieve it. This book is not a one-size-fits-all guide to healing, as no book or healing modality is. In the same way I invite my clients to try different exercises in and out of the therapy room, I invite you to play around with various exercises and see what works for you. The worksheets provided help make the guide even more practical; use them! Whether you have struggled with mild or more severe forms of anxiety, you will learn ways to increase your well-being and personal growth.

The simple truth is this: we cannot escape the reality of being human in an ever-changing world, but we can manage the experiences, reactions, and emotions that surface within our mind and body. Once you have acquired the right tools to get your anxiety under control, you open yourself to feeling joyful and ready to live your best life.

Now that's what I call living freely.

—Nadine Macaluso, Ph.D.

INTRODUCTION

Anxiety has ripped through my life.

I have spent the past 10 plus years trying everything under the sun to try to help my daughter, and myself, get through our mutual anxiety. At times it was so bad that I did not even feel that I would make it through the day. I felt like I was watching a movie of everyone else living their lives, but we couldn't live ours because we were prisoners of anxiety.

It stopped us from traveling, going to school, seeing friends, and celebrating holidays. Anxiety kept us isolated and feeling alone. The ironic thing is for the past 30 years I have been coaching and writing popular self-help books and helping everyone else with their lives, but I didn't even realize how much anxiety was negatively affecting my life.

Even though my daughter was the main person suffering from anxiety, I too was suffering from anxiety and post-traumatic stress. Until one day I talked to my best friend who just happens to be an amazing therapist, and she helped me understand anxiety on a whole different level.

I had been trying to deal with anxiety as if it was logical, but anxiety is not logical. It's primal and cannot be rationalized. My best friend helped me realize that in order to manage mine and my daughter's anxiety, we were going to have to look it in the eye and go through the discomfort of it. Going through the anxiety was the only way out of the vicious cycle. The most amazing thing she taught me was that when anxiety is high, it is absolutely essential to calm the body down first, before you can begin to solve any kind of problem.

Today the word "anxiety" is everywhere: kids, teens, adults, older adults, men, women, and the numbers are increasing. There are currently 40 million adults, if not more, in the United States alone that are suffering from anxiety. Sadly only 37 percent of people get help. The other 63 percent suffer silently.

It is my passion in writing this self-help book to inspire many more people to push through their challenges with anxiety. To give people hope and understanding so that they too can take charge of their anxiety, rather than feeling like their anxiety is controlling them.

When I first started researching the subject of anxiety and looked at what books were out there, I found lots of academic books and lots of coaching books, but I did not find any self-helps books that walked people through the entire process in a down-to-earth format. That is why I created *The Instant Anxiety Solution*.

I am a best-selling author of a self-help book on pregnancy fitness. I am passionate about helping people improve their lives for the better. I have helped hundreds of thousands of women around the world achieve better health and wellness through my books and newsletters. I have a master's degree in Holistic Nutrition, a bachelor's degree in Psychology and a Certificate in Kinesiology's Health and Fitness Studies. I have studied and been mentored extensively on the subject of anxiety, I have coached people in addictions recovery and mental health, I have a lot of experience with emotional dysregulations and sensory processing issues and a lot of experience empowering people to change their behavior. But most importantly, I am someone who gets it. I have struggled with anxiety, lived through caring for someone with severe anxiety, and managed to get us to the other side where anxiety is now manageable, where we are living and loving life to the fullest and we can breathe a lot easier.

Today I'm going to share with you all the amazing things that I learned along the way. This book is a compilation of my training, teaching, education, coaching, mentoring and breakthroughs. And now I'm fast-tracking the process for you. I've simplified the solution in to a 5-step formula that will change your relationship with anxiety, and as a result, change your life.

The Instant Anxiety Solution is an essential read for every person suffering from anxiety. Just like my best friend helped me, I am going to help you. Regardless of where you are at on the spectrum of anxiety, this book can help you move forward by providing you with new practical information and steps to manage your anxiety better.

Give yourself time to work through and learn your new skills. You are re-learning ingrained patterns and behaviors that will take time to unlearn, so be easy on yourself and give yourself time to go through the process. There are worksheets at the back of the book to help you out.

Okay, let's do this. Let's begin your journey!

DISCLAIMER

This book is for education purposes only. It is *not* therapy. This book is a combination of my journey, experience, training and education. This book is a generalized program for the mass population. Please ask your doctor or therapist about any concept or exercise that you want to try in this book *before* you take action. **You doctor knows you and your situation best.** They are the only ones to give you advice. Depending on how deeply rooted your anxiety is, you may need to seek out help from a professional to work through some of your personal issues.

CHAPTER 1

ANXIETY RE-WIRED

People with anxiety have great difficulty staying in the present moment, often projecting their past worries and fears into the present (and the future).

In my 30-year journey of coaching and empowering people, I've come to realize that anxiety is very much the **fear of the future** and a **fear of the unknown**. It is a fear of "what if" or "what could be" that is keeping us stressed and feeing stuck.

Many of us wonder what causes anxiety. Why does one person get it and the other does not?

The cause of anxiety is both nature and nurture. Some of us are naturally wired to be more anxious than others, while others of us grew up in a more "anxiety provoked" environment.

Can Someone Be More Genetically Wired for Anxiety?

Yes, someone can be more genetically wired for anxiety. But anxiety is not caused ONLY as a result of biological makeup. Chemicals are always changing. Several other things contribute to causing anxiety. Sometimes we learn it from a parent. Sometimes it is the lack of structure and routine that make us feel unsafe. Sometimes it is being ignored or told we "Should be stronger" that makes us not trust ourselves. And not learning how to manage our emotions effectively when growing up plays a profound role with anxiety. As you can see, various stressors can add to the genetic predisposition causing us to have anxiety.

Other factors that can contribute to anxiety are:

- Built up/reoccurring stress
- Lack of sleep/exhaustion
- Trauma
- System on overdrive

- Highly sensitive personality
- Trouble asserting self
- Poor emotional regulation
- Social media usage
- Unsupportive upbringing
- Neglectful upbringing
- Criticism and put down
- Living in chaos, unstructured environment
- Blood relatives with anxiety
- Illness
- Stressful homelife or relationship
- Financial difficulties

Neurotransmitter Imbalance

Lack of sleep, over-working, over-exercising, and negative relationships contribute to neurotransmitter imbalances. Neurotransmitters are the signaling chemicals in our brains that are responsible for things like our mood, motivation, and energy level. When our neurotransmitters become unbalanced, we experience things like depression and anxiety, lack of motivation, stress, burnout, and memory problems.

Serotonin is the neurotransmitter associated with emotion and mood. Low serotonin is found to be common in people who suffer from depression and social anxiety disorders. Symptoms of low serotonin include feelings of unhappiness, dissatisfaction, indifference, frustration, and anger.

Most of the serotonin in our bodies is made in the gut first. **If your gut health is poor, then your body is less capable of converting amino acids from food into the neurotransmitters in your brain.** Research shows that eating the right kind of fat, in the right quantities, can help increase energy, speed up metabolism, and reduce anxiety and depression. Linoleic fatty acids (omega-3) and linolenic fatty acids (omega-6) are required to consume, since the body cannot produce them on their own.

Essential fats increase the efficient delivery of oxygen and nutrients to the tissues by increasing the flexibility of the red blood cell membranes and making the insides of arteries more slippery. These good fats increase the production of haemoglobin, which also increases the amount of oxygen available to cells, an essential factor in improving your mood. You can get your essential fats from things like flaxseed oil, hempseed oil, and walnut oil. Increasing fatty fish like Alaskan salmon, is also a good idea.

What are some common symptoms of anxiety?

- Nausea
- Increased worry
- Increased fearfulness
- High stress
- Lump in throat
- Choking feeling
- Nervous/on edge
- Agitated
- Difficulty focusing
- Not being able to sit still
- Trouble falling asleep
- Poor interrupted sleep
- Headaches

- Shaking
- Muscle tightness
- Sweating
- Stomach upset
- Diarrhea
- Irritable
- Trouble relaxing
- Loss of appetite
- Binge eating
- Skipping meals
- Racing heart
- Difficulty focusing and paying attention

Sleep and Anxiety

The National Institute of Neurological Disorders and Stroke report that 40 million people in the United States suffer from chronic long-term sleep disorders each year. It is no surprise that the same reported number of people that suffer from anxiety each year also suffer from sleep disorders. Anxiety and sleep disorders go hand in hand. Anxiety can cause sleep difficulty and sleep deprivation can cause anxiety. The problem worsens as lack of sleep causes us to be further disconnected from our emotions. And once we are disconnected from our emotions, our anxiety gets worse. It is currently estimated that 1 in 4 people experience sleep difficulty, including trouble falling asleep, staying asleep, early morning waking, restless and unsatisfying sleep. In fact, a sleepless night is known to cause a rise in anxiety by 30 percent.

Poor or no sleep causes people to become more irritable, feel depressed, and causes them to be unable to think properly. Sleep problems affects how we function emotionally, mentally, and physically. Add to that a lack of support and understanding from those around us, which makes the situation worse, and when anxiety gets bad, insomnia can set in. Which is terrible as I know first-hand with my daughter. She could stay up for a week at a time without sleeping and not be able to come down to rest at all. It was like watching the Energizer Bunny, keep going and going.

It's important to create a sleep schedule and sleep routine. Try to avoid exercise in the evening, it will keep you too stimulated causing difficulty relaxing. Also avoid watching the news or a violent movie before bed. The same thing goes for caffeine and alcohol, they have been known to work against a good night's sleep. Focus on creating a nice, calming sleep routine like having a warm glass of milk or your favorite tea, take a nice long hot bath, listen to relaxing music and read a nice book before bed. Start your sleep routine a good hour or two before you want to go to sleep.

There are a lot of natural insomnia/sleep aids out there to help relieve your symptoms. Melatonin and Magnesium are good supplements to look into. Magnesium helps the body relax and sleep longer. Melatonin on the other hand, helps you fall asleep faster. If you need something stronger to help you sleep, talk to your doctor.

How does anxiety affect quality of life?

- Excessive worry
- Poor concentration
- Overwhelm
- Headaches
- Depression

- Social withdrawal
- Feeling hopeless
- Panic attacks
- Irritability
- Stomach upset
- Shortness of breath
- Chest tightness
- Heart palpitations
- Loss of libido
- Muscle aches and pains
- Exhaustion
- Increased blood pressure
- Sleep problems
- Isolation

Social Media Dangers

Anxiety is compounded by the use of social media. These platforms at their core are designed to be addictive, making us "need" to come back for more, constantly checking in, measuring up, comparing ourselves to others, seeing what other people are doing and counting how many people like or respond to our posts.

If you think of it this way, social media, just like food or sex, activates the brain's reward centre by releasing the chemical dopamine, the "feel-good chemical," when things are good. Social media also has the ability to negatively affect our mood, self-esteem and feeling of worthiness, by being judged and not being included, all heightening our state of anxiety.

According to the PEW Research Centre, 69 percent of adults and 81 percent of teens use social media. The younger the person starts using social media, the greater the impact the platforms have on their mental health. Social media puts a distorted lens on appearances and reality. The dependency, the constant connectedness, the unrealistic expectations, the FOMO (fear of missing out), the "false reality", the use of filters and editing features, makes the social media world also very dangerous and a risky place for our mental health.

Social media also increases the opportunity for aggressive behaviors like excluding others and writing hurtful comments, leaving people feeling unsafe, and like they don't fit in or measure up.

Put Your Oxygen Mask on First

If you're helping someone with anxiety, the most important lesson is to put your own oxygen mask on first. This is a critical lesson and one that took me many years to understand. For years I kept insisting on helping my daughter first before I took care of myself. I wanted to put her oxygen mask on before mine. But we all know what will happen if I get her mask on before I get a chance to put my own mask on in an emergency situation. That's right, I'll run out of air. Bottom line is, you can't help anyone if you can't help yourself first. You must be healthy and strong to help someone else through their anxiety. If your gas tank is on "empty" you cannot be of much help to anyone, so it is time to take care of yourself now. Do things to "fill up" your gas tank.

CHAPTER 2

SOUNDING THE
A.L.A.R.M.

A.L.A.R.M. is the acronym to "kick into action" whenever you start to feel anxious: Activate, Label, Acknowledge, Remember, and Move Forward.

Whenever you START to feel anxious, sound the A.L.A.R.M. immediately:

1. **Activate** your parasympathetic nervous system.

2. **Label** your emotion.

3. **Acknowledge** emotions are temporary.

4. **Remember** to avoid adding on extra thoughts and emotions to your original, true emotion.

5. **Move forward**, problem solve and take action.

Activate Your Parasympathetic Nervous System

To reduce anxiety, the first thing you MUST do is calm your sympathetic nervous system down. Get your body out of "the acute stress" stage and into a calmer state so you can think properly.

When we experience anxiety, the body goes into a "fight or flight" mode. When we get triggered by an event, our amygdala gets activated, causing the impulsive fight or flight response and the prefrontal cortex, the logical thinking part of the brain, shuts off. When anxious, physiologically our body shuts down our thinking capability and prepares you for one thing only, for survival.

After the amygdala gets triggered, it causes the sympathetic nervous system to get "activated" causing your heart rate, breathing, and blood pressure to rise dramatically. You'll notice a pounding in your chest, an increased heart rate, increased breathing rate, and sweating. You'll likely even feel shaky and nauseous.

Many people make the mistake of trying to problem solve when anxiety hits, but it is *absolutely* impossible to do. **As a rule, you cannot think until your body is calmed down, until you have "activated" your parasympathetic nervous system (PSNS), the calming part of your nervous system.**

If you think of it this way, the sympathetic nervous system acts like the "gas pedal" in the car, speeding the car up to high speeds to get you out of danger, like "putting the peddle to the metal." The parasympathetic nervous system on the other hand, does the complete opposite, it acts to "slow you down" and calm your body and mind, like putting the "breaks on."

> Learning how to shock the body (and mind) out of its highly anxious state and "activate" the parasympathetic nervous system is a highly useful skill that can be used to manage anxiety and other strong emotions.

Many people have an underactive parasympathetic nervous system and overactive sympathetic nervous system. To take control of anxiety, we must learn to activate our parasympathetic nervous system on demand.

The goal is to find a handful of strategies that work for you to quickly activate your PSNS and bring about a different physical and emotional reaction. There is not a one size fits all solution. Something that works for you may not work for someone else. Once you find what works for you, it's a good idea to practice doing these strategies on a regular basis so that when you **really** need them to work, the reaction will be automatic in helping you relax quickly. For example, eventually when you smell something that pleases you, it will automatically bring you to your "happy place." For me, when I pull my ear back, I instantly relax (I explain more about this later).

Learning to take control of your nervous system is one of the greatest gifts and the vagal nerve is your secret.

The vagal nerve is the **main cranial nerve in the parasympathetic nervous system,** carrying important sensory and motor information from the brain to the gut and vice versa. It connects the heart, esophagus, lungs, blood vessels, abdomen, and colon. It is responsible for helping you handle stress better and regulating your mood. It is how you develop resilience and emotional well-being. It is also responsible for the involuntary functions of the body like breathing, swallowing, speech, digestion, circulation, and elimination. But the most important function of the vagal nerve is getting you back to a state of calm **after** a stressful event.

Think of the vagal nerve as your body's own **feedback mechanism** that communicates to the brain that it is safe to relax and de-stress. It delivers critical interoceptive information to the brain like temperature, pressure, and pain. When it gets activated, it sends signals to the brain that it is okay to slow down the heart rate and blood pressure allowing the body to relax.

High vagal tone means the body can return to a calm state quickly after a stressful event ends. Low vagal tone means it takes the body a long time to return to a calm state after stress. The goal is to train your body to have high vagal tone. The best way to do this is to do "vagal exercises" to activate it regularly. The more time you spend in a high PSNS state, the healthier you will feel.

In some instances, the sympathetic nervous system remains chronically active due to lifestyle, poor habits, and toxic stress, never allowing the parasympathetic nervous system to do its job of rest, digest and relax. As a result, the individual stays in a permanent state of chronic stress causing problems like anxiety, insomnia, digestive issues, inflammation, fatigue, heart palpitations, hormonal imbalance, panic attacks and more.

The first thing I notice when my vagal nerve gets stimulated is I automatically take a **huge breath of air—** and it is the most amazing feeling. My chest feels like it completely opens up. Another sign I've noticed when my vagal nerve gets activated is a big yawn.

There are two specific exercises that I find quick and effective at "helping you out" when you are experiencing **high anxiety**, or you just want to shift your emotional state. I applied this technique the other day when I was "feeling anxious," and within 30 minutes, I felt like a new person. These wonderful exercises shock the body, distract the mind, and quickly alter the way you feel. The deep breathing technique afterwards further activated my parasympathetic nervous system to help calm me down even more.

Temperature Change

Cold exposure is a great way to **quickly activate your parasympathetic nervous system** and "cool" the body AND mind down when you are experiencing high anxiety. The cold **tricks** the body to slow down physiologically and mentally distracts the mind from the stress of anxiety.

When we're upset, our bodies and minds are "hot." **What we want to do is dramatically change the body's temperature by shocking the system.** If you imagine yourself jumping into a freezing cold pool, despite the shock of it, remember how refreshed and calm you felt afterwards? This is the feeling that you want.

Jumping in a cold shower, splashing icy water on your face, or putting a cold pack on the back of your neck, will immediately shock your body and activate your vagal nerve.

Quick temperature change also acts as a great mindfulness technique. The cold instantaneously distracts the mind and gets your attention away from your stressor.

Aim to find something quick and very cold to "surprise" your system. Make sure to do it long enough that it will make you feel that "shock" or "surprise", but not too long that you will hurt yourself.

Here are some examples:

- Take a really cold shower.
- Jump in a cold pool or lake.
- Splash icy cold water on your face 5-10 times.
- Put an ice pack on the back of your neck.
- Hold an ice cube for 30 seconds to 1 minute.
- Put air conditioning on your face full blast.
- Put your hand in a bucket of ice water.

Intense Exercise

When you are feeling really wound up, intense exercise can be helpful to immediately calm your body down. When your body is in a highly triggered SNS state, doing exercise **to exhaustion**, will kick the PSNS in. "Intense" exercise SHOCKS the body by drastically increasing oxygen in the body and dramatically decreasing your stress level. It also quickly distracts the mind by having to be 100 percent focused on the activity you're doing and away from the stress.

Note: Please check with your doctor BEFORE you do these or any of the exercises in this book to make sure it is okay for you to do. My suggestions are generalized for education only.

1. Sprint to the end of the block.

2. Do push ups until you reach exhaustion.

3. Do jumping jacks or burpees until you reach exhaustion.

4. Jump in the pool and swim as fast as you can for a few laps.

If you're NOT really stressed out, but still want to calm down, focus on doing low to moderate aerobic exercise that you enjoy.

The most natural way to change your brain chemistry is to exercise. Exercise provides a similar benefit to anti-depressant medication, without the side effects. Exercise has been proven to reduce cortisol and adrenaline levels, reducing anxiety.

Exercise also releases endorphins and other neuro-chemicals which help improve our mood and give us a heightened sense of well-being.

> I like to add a half block sprint in the middle of my walk if I'm having an intense emotion or repetitive thoughts–it works perfectly to distract my mind.

When we exercise, the body gets flooded with an increase in serotonin, dopamine, and norepinephrine. Less cortisol and more dopamine mean self-regulation is much easier and you will cope better with stressful situations that come up throughout the day. Serotonin is responsible for feelings of serenity and hopefulness. Dopamine and Norepinephrine are responsible for feelings of relaxation and happiness.

> Research has found that a 20-minute workout can produce altered mood benefits that can last up to 12 hours.

If you can exercise in the morning, the endorphins released will improve your mood throughout the day, helping you to better cope with stressful situations that come up.

Morning exercise is also a good way to beat procrastination and avoidance. Planning activities with a friend or joining a class can provide extra motivation.

What Kind of Exercise Are We Talking About?

Doing exercise does not necessarily mean you have to join a gym, go to a spin class, or take up running. Many benefits of exercise are found at the lower intensity level. **That means going for a brisk walk is an excellent choice for exercise.** To increase the intensity, which will help you feel even better mentally and physically, you can add in a hill or two. You can even add in a light jog for a half a block or more, every few minutes. Interval training is an excellent form of exercise that allows you to increase your heart rate for short periods of time. You will be amazed at how your fitness level and endurance will quickly improve when you add in a jog or a hill to your brisk walk.

Be mindful of your body as you walk. Notice how it feels, your breathing, your blood circulating, your heart rate rising. Notice the environment around you, the sky, the landscape, the terrain. Breath in the air. Concentrate on lengthening and deepening your breaths.

If you are just beginning to incorporate exercise in your daily routine, start with an easy routine; a difficult or strenuous regimen may be too hard to maintain.

Your optimal goal is to get 15–20 minutes (or more) of cardiovascular activity 3–5 days a week. On other days, focus on being active as much as you can—even if it is just for a few minutes—you will feel much better about yourself.

As a rule, if you can sing while you are exercising, your activity is too easy; if your speech is a bit labored, but you can still communicate, you are exercising at the right level. This is called the Talk Test.

Track Your Steps

Tracking your steps is a great motivator. You can put on a pedometer or use your phone app to track how many steps you take per day.

Pedometers are designed to count the number of steps a person takes, as opposed to the number of miles walked. There is no right or wrong number. **The goal is to gradually increase the number of steps you take per day**. You can do this by taking an extra walk every day, parking in the back of the parking lot instead of the front, walking up the stairs instead of taking the elevator, or going for longer walks (this is ideal as it will help you burn more fat). Keep your tracker on all day and try to add in little bits of activity as much as you can, whenever you can. It is inspiring to see how many steps you've taken in a day. You will notice a quick improvement in your stamina over a short period of time. My personal goal is to take 10,000 steps at day. What is your number?

The Dive Response

The dive response is another great exercise when you need a quick solution to strong emotion. We all know how SHOCKING it is to put your hand, face or body in freezing cold water. I was reminded of this just the other day when our power went out in my house and within 15 seconds, I was having a freezing cold, unbearable shower.

If immersing your head in icy cold water doesn't appeal to you, you can activate the "dive response" by simply holding an ice pack or zip-loc bag full of ice, freezing cold water, or frozen peas to your eyes or cheeks while at the **same time**, hold your breath—it's amazing, your body will think you are under water! This "underwater trick" will **immediately** slow down all of your body systems and calm you down as if you were underwater. Your heart and breathing will slow down immediately, and the blood will be directed to the brain and heart and you will feel calm.

> The dive response is a great way to manage intense emotion when you need a quick solution to strong emotion.

Ear Massage

Your ears are the magic gateway to your vagal nerve and the parasympathetic nervous system. Simple ear exercises can activate the PSNS and calm you down quickly. See which one, if any, work for you.

Here are some exercises to try:

- Pull the ears slightly back away from your skull, upwards, backward and downwards.

- Put your finger in the ear crease above the canal and gently make circular motions for 30 seconds.

- Put your finger inside your ear canal towards the back of your head and do gentle circle motions for 30 seconds.

- Put your finger behind your ear, between the ear and the hairline, and gently pull the skin backwards or in circular motions. Maintain each exercise for 30 seconds.

- Tapping gently behind your ear also stimulates the PSNS.

Humming or Singing

The vagal nerve surrounds our voice box, or larynx, and when stimulated, activates your PSNS. Humming,

Om-ing and singing are excellent ways to activate your vagal nerve and calm you down when you are feeling stressed or anxious.

Humming, Om-ing and singing provide vibrations that massage the section of your vagal nerve near your vocal cords to activate the PSNS and tell your body you are safe. Put the volume up and sing loud and proud. You do not have to be a professional singer to reap the rewards of singing on the nervous system.

NOTE: Gargling is another way to activate your vagal nerve. Closing the throat muscles activates the vagal nerve.

The Power of a Good Scream

One of my favorite ways to change my brain chemistry naturally and quickly, is to SCREAM!! Sometimes when I'm feeling stressed, I get an intense need to scream, and it works wonderfully! In fact, screaming is such an effective tool they even have therapies centered on screaming.

If you feel your tension building and could benefit from "getting it out" and releasing your pent-up emotions, do it. A good scream is an excellent cathartic release—often releasing endorphins afterwards like with a runner's high. If you don't want to scream freely, you can try screaming in a pillow. A silent scream even does the trick.

Give it a try, you just may feel better afterwards!

Deep Breathing

A deep sigh or yawn is your body's **natural way** to **release tension** and **reset your nervous system**. You can even activate this response by "yawning."

Deep breathing also works wonders to activate the PSNS by allowing your body to slow down and reset. Typically, we breathe in around 12-14 times a minute, it's good practice to slow your breathing down to 6 times (or less) a minute to reduce stress and anxiety. Concentrate on breathing deeply down into your diaphragm, expand your stomach, with deep inhales and slow, long exhales. This will help to reduce your body's fight or flight stress response and reduce emotional pain.

If you'd like a more structured breathing technique to slow your breathing down, inhale for a count of 4, hold for a count of 4, and then exhale for a count of 4 or even 6 if you can. Repeat.

Progressive Muscle Relaxation

Progressive Muscle Relaxation is another great way to relax your body and mind. Progressive muscle relaxation is a two-step process of tensing and then relaxing your muscles. The idea is to put your "mind in your muscle", one muscle group at a time. To try this, tense a group of muscles, hold for 5 seconds, and then relax the muscle. Work your way from the top of your body down, one muscle group at a time, or vice versa.

You will notice that after doing the tension and release, the muscles will become more relaxed than they were before they were tightened, and you will feel more relaxed. **Relaxed muscles require less oxygen which allows your breathing and heart rate to slow down and you to feel calmer**. Progressive muscle relaxation is a great way to take charge of your body and mind. The better you become at this exercise, the quicker you will be able to access the "relaxation response" when you really need it.

Set aside about 10 minutes to complete this exercise. It's best to find a quiet place to do this exercise to really get in touch with your body.

Increase Your Vagal Tone by Activating Your Senses

Activating your senses, activates your vagal nerve, and creates a "pleasurable" PSNS state. This will allow you to self-soothe and calm down both physically and mentally on DEMAND.

- **Activate Your Sense of Taste.** Chew your favorite gum, eat your favorite food, suck on a favorite sour candy. Something to "wake up" your taste buds and add a pep to your taste sense.

- **Activate Your Sense of Sight.** Look at an image of something you love, like an old picture of a favorite place, person or event. Find something that brings you pleasure and helps you feel peaceful.

- **Active Your Sense of Smell.** Put on your favorite lip balm, hand cream, perfume or burn your favorite candle. Smell has a way of making us feel better. Find a smell that you love.

- **Activate Your Sense of Touch.** Take a warm bubble bath, get a relaxing massage, or put flavoured lip gloss on (my favorite!)—touching the lips will immediately activate the PSNS.

- **Activate Your Sense of Hearing.** Play your favorite song or call a supportive friend. I find turning the music up loud inspires me and makes me feel better, especially when I add some loud singing to go with it. Find something that works for you.

- **Activate Your Kinesthetic/Proprioception.** Put on a weighted blanket or weighted vest, get a deep hug from a loved one, swing on a swing, or dance around the house.

Proprioception

Proprioception is one of the senses and involves self-movement and body position. This sense is responsible for balance, pressure and knowing where the body parts are in space in relation to the other parts. For example, being able to coordinate the body to move as one unit, and in relation to its parts, like being able to touch your finger to your nose. For many this sounds like an incredibly simple task, but for those with weak proprioceptive awareness, this is a difficult task.

Most of the receptors are in the muscles, joints and tendons. When you move or feel pressure, the receptors send signals to the brain. It is a complex sense that allows us to perceive the body's position and body in space. Having good proprioception helps reduce the risk of injury. **Poor proprioception would be bumping into things, being clumsy, or being accident prone.**

When someone experiences brain damage and they try to hold an egg, it is very difficult. Not knowing how hard to squeeze is an example of an "injured sense of proprioception."

To calm the proprioception sense or connect the person to their body, deep pressure works great. Weighted blankets, weighted vests or weighted jackets work great. Strong hugs also do the magic! They will instantly provide a feeling of calm, safety and security.

Some other good ideas that distract the mind are:

1. Play with a paddle ball or yo-yo

2. Play with an animal

3. Walk in nature

4. Exercise

5. Hug an animal

6. Sit and relax in the sun

7. Say the alphabet backwards

8. Dance around the house

9. Change your posture (opening your posture will change how you feel)

10. Turn the music up in your car and sing loud

These will get you to concentrate on the task, distract your mind and bring your emotional intensity level down.

Other Ways to Change Your Brain Chemistry

Food and Anxiety

When using a holistic approach to anxiety, we must also look at how our food affects our anxiety level. In general, **a diet rich in whole grains, beans and legumes, fruits and vegetables is the best way to eat**. We want to avoid simple sugars, processed and packaged food, and white flour products as much as possible, they are full of empty calories, high sodium, loaded with nasty preservatives and cause our blood sugar levels to rise and fall, leaving us exposed to mood swings.

Focus on eating foods rich in magnesium to keep you calm. Concentrate on eating whole grains, legumes, nuts, seeds and green leafy vegetables. It's also a good idea to add avocados and almonds to your diet, these foods are rich in B vitamins and help improve your mood. Antioxidants are also excellent to add to your regimen, try adding cranberries, strawberries, raspberries or blueberries to your salads or yogurt.

Taking a good probiotic every day is also important for optimal health. They say the "gut is the second brain," influencing our mood and well-being. We have to make sure we pay attention to our gut health and a good probiotic is the best way to do that.

> To properly digest and absorb your nutrients, the parasympathetic nervous system (PSNS) must be activated.

Water and Health

Drink lots of water every day. Many of us neglect to drink an adequate amount of water each day and exist in a state of semi-dehydration. We also very often confuse hunger with thirst and eat instead of drink.

You will be able to improve your physical and mental health by increasing the amount of water that you drink throughout the day. To stay properly hydrated, you need to drink approximately 8 cups of water a day or more if you are exercising or the weather is hot, and you are perspiring. Add a squeeze of lemon juice or have hot water with lemon to help get your 8 glasses a day.

It is recommended that you drink between meals, as drinking too much water during or after a meal, dilutes the digestive enzymes and slows down the absorption of nutrients.

Signs of dehydration include:

- Bad breath
- Dry skin
- Headache
- Infrequent need to urinate and dark urine
- Sticky saliva
- Weakness and fatigue

CHAPTER 3

LABELING "WHAT" YOU ARE FEELING

We are all born with the biological predisposition to experience emotions. Emotions are a natural and healthy part of our survival. Emotions alert us to danger by providing a physiological reaction to a physical or mental threat. Emotions also provide us with important information about our inside world, connecting us to the deepest parts of ourselves.

When an emotion gets validated, or confirmed, and someone listens to you, the emotional intensity will go down. The opposite is also true, the emotion will grow in intensity when you go to communicate about an emotion and nobody listens to you, or you feel invalidated. This is especially true when we judge ourselves or invalidate our own emotion by saying "I shouldn't feel this way" or someone else invalidates your emotion by saying "you shouldn't feel this way."

The interesting point about emotions, even negative ones, is that they are NOT bad. Anxiety is NOT bad. In fact, without a little anxiety, we would have a hard time getting out of bed in the morning and doing our daily tasks. Anxiety motivates us to go about our day, to get to work on time, to finish our homework, to pay our taxes, to buy groceries, and to pick up the kids.

The goal is to have some anxiety, so you are motivated to get to work on time and get your homework done by deadline, but not so much that it interferes with your day-to-day functioning. It goes back to the foundation, where anxiety serves a purpose. Anxiety is the element that makes us motivated to wake up in the morning, to start our day, to get to work on time, hand in our assignment on time, to remember a special birthday, to buy groceries for dinner. It motivates us to go about our daily activities. If we didn't have any "care" or "motivation" we wouldn't get up in the morning, we wouldn't go to work or school, we wouldn't get our homework or work done.

Rather than try to make anxiety go away, what we want to do is learn **how to keep anxiety at the level that motivates us to get things done but doesn't interfere with our quality of life**. We want to learn skills and techniques so we can feel like we are "on top" of our anxiety, rather than our anxiety being on "top of us."

There are seven original emotions:

1. Anxiety/Fear

2. Anger

3. Sadness

4. Guilt

5. Shame

6. Love

7. Happiness

The Difference Between Shame and Guilt

Shame and guilt have overlapping qualities that often lead us to confuse these two emotions. Although they both have the same biological urges—**wanting to hide**—they are very different.

Guilt is when your emotion "fits" with your values. Shame is when your emotion "does NOT fit" with your values. With guilt, the **impulse** is often that you **want to say sorry**. **Shame** on the other hand, **brings up a lot of feelings of inadequacy, not feeling good enough**. Shame is a very common emotion.

Label Your Feelings

The first step in learning to take charge of your anxiety is to **put a label or name to your emotion**. As soon as you can IDENTIFY what you are feeling, you will have a much better chance of solving your problem and decreasing your emotional intensity.

Labeling your emotion is being AWARE of what you are feeling. **You do not need to know WHY you feel a certain way, just acknowledge WHAT you feel, so that you can begin to move on.**

Emotions are different from thoughts in that they take the form of one word. If I say, for example, "I feel like you don't care," that is a thought. If I say, "I feel sad," the sadness is the emotion.

Emotions Are Not Always Right

A very interesting point I learned along my journey is that emotions are not always right. They serve a biological purpose but sometimes what we are feeling, although it feels very real, **does not match the situation.** For example, you can be scared because you heard a loud noise when you were walking alone in a dark alley. You can also be the same level of scared when you are standing in front of a crowd of people.

To better understand what we are feeling, we can look to our ACTION IMPULSES for information. Action Impulses are powerful, immediate CLUES as to what is going on inside of us. These "impulses" tell us a lot about ourselves and what we are feeling.

For example, if you hear a noise when you are walking in an alley, you RUN. The action impulse to RUN protects you from danger. The same action impulse might happen when you stand in front of an audience to speak. You might have that same **IMPULSE** to run or bolt when you see the crowd. In this case, the "appropriateness" of the emotional reaction does NOT match the situation.

If the "action response" does not match the "appropriateness" of the situation, you can learn to change HOW you respond to the situation. For example, you can teach yourself to not be so afraid of standing in front of a crowd by practicing speaking in front of small groups.

It is amazing how intuitive the body is. Once you learn to read the "secret language of emotions," you will have a much easier time managing your mood.

Here's a list of common action impulses:

1. You feel like you want to **HIDE** = you are likely feeling **sad or down, shame or embarrassed.**

2. You feel like you want to **RUN** or **AVOID** the situation = you are likely feeling **anxious.**

3. You want to **ATTACK, YELL, PUNCH** = you are likely feeling **angry.**

4. You want to **WITHDRAW** or **HIDE** or want to **APOLOGIZE** = you are likely feeling **guilt.**

5. You want to **ISOLATE** and **WITHDRAW** = you are likely feeling **sad.**

Interoceptive Awareness

Interoception is **the sense of "knowing" or "feeling" what is going on inside your body**, including the internal organs and skin. Some people have high body awareness, others have poor body awareness. This awareness includes being in touch with your hunger, thirst, pain, arousal, bowel and bladder, heart rate, breathing, sweating, etc.

The ability to manage our emotions effectively involves the ability to accurately detect and evaluate internal cues to stressful events. Poor or disrupted Interoception makes emotional regulation very difficult.

Sit back and close your eyes:

- Is your heart beating fast or slow?

- Do you feel hungry or full?

- Do you feel tired or energized?

These are just some simple ways of noticing if you're connected to what is going on internally in your body. When we tune in, most of us are able to accurately connect to this sense called **interoception**. Little receptors in the skin, muscles, and bones and organs send information about our internal state to our brain to be interpreted.

Often the sensors in the body let us know how we're feeling. For example, breathing rapidly, elevated heart rate, or excessive sweating would tell us that we're feeling anxious or nervous about the situation that we are in, or anticipating.

When the interoception system is working well, the information notifies us of our internal environment so we can take appropriate action and solve the problem. For example, take a natural stress remedy if you're feeling anxious, eat when you are hungry, drink when you are thirsty, take your jacket off if you are feeling hot.

Interoception not only affects our ability to self-regulate, but it is also associated with important skills like self-awareness, intuition, social interaction, and problem-solving abilities.

Sometimes there is "disconnect" and for some reason or another, the brain does not properly interpret the information correctly or the person does not act on the information correctly. I see this a lot with special needs, especially autism. But it doesn't just happen with special needs. It happens in the neuro-typical population as well. Some of us are more connected to our bodies than those who "over-ride" the urge and keep the disconnect going.

I just sat with an old friend of mine who said she once realized that she did not urinate for 28-hours. She was so disconnected from her body that she didn't get a signal that she needed to go, and when she did, she over-rode the urge by telling herself that she "did not have time." Next thing she knew she had gone over a day without urinating, and she was in excruciating pain.

Many of us are not as extreme as my friend, but we do spend most of our day not attending or not being connected to our bodies. We sit at the computer, work at our desk, talk on the phone and run errands, disconnected from what we are feeling inside our bodies. We rarely give our body any attention. **Good health and emotional management are dependent on us being aware of our body.**

Imagine if you notice yourself getting really uncomfortable and agitated but don't know why?

You can feel yourself getting irritated and run down but don't realize that it is because your stomach is growling, and you haven't eaten for 8 hours.

The more attention we give to our bodies, the better it is. **The more self-aware we become, the better we are able to manage our lives and stay on top of our stress and anxiety**. The more we work on noticing how our bodies are feeling, the better we'll be able to operate in the world and increase our resilience.

Helping to improve our sensory and bodily awareness will help reduce stress, improve emotional regulation, and help us feel healthier. It is a good idea to check in daily with how you are feeling.

Ask yourself, do I have . . .

- Neck or headache?

- Tight shoulders or face?

- Stomach ache?

- Twitching?

- Sore neck, back or hips?

- Sore eyes, feet or legs?

- Do I feel tension anywhere (shoulders, hips, back)?

CHAPTER 4

ACKNOWLEDGE THAT EMOTIONS ARE TEMPORARY

Emotions only last up to seven minutes.
Meaning every seven minutes, you have
an opportunity to change the way you feel
and not be a prisoner of your emotion.

My brilliant friend taught me this concept, that emotions are temporary. When we get a strong emotion, we get flooded with intensity and it feels like it is going to last forever, making it very hard to manage. But the good news is, **emotions last up to 7 minutes**

ONLY and then they are done. Yep, although it feels like the emotion will last forever, it won't. Emotions are NOT continuous.

Even though things like "sadness" or "anger" feel like they stay around for a long time, it is because we **attach additional thoughts and emotions to the original emotion**. If you think of it this way, you feel the emotion strongly for the first 7 minutes or less and then it runs out of steam on its own. It's the additional energy that is added in the form of our "extra" thoughts and emotions that we "attach" to the original emotion that keeps the feeling alive and the suffering occurring.

Emotions are very much temporary. They come and they go. We don't laugh for a half an hour. We laugh for a short time. We don't cry for a half an hour; we cry for a little time. Same thing with feeling anxious. So, if we can think of emotions as temporary feelings, we can see that the emotions don't define us.

In fact, every 7 minutes, you have an opportunity to change the way you feel. For example, when you are angry or anxious, the **emotion seems to last an exceptionally long time, almost like you are drowning in it, but know with 100 percent confidence, that you will ALWAYS come up for air to catch your breath**.

Every seven minutes or less, your emotion will expire. Your head, even though it might feel like it will, does not stay underwater. You naturally come up to catch a breath every 7 minutes. Whether its anger, anxiety, or sadness, they all expire. You will NOT keep feeling the emotion.

So next time you feel a negative emotion, comfort yourself in knowing that the feeling is only temporary. It is the thoughts that we attach to the emotions that we need to work on. **Learning how to stop layering your thoughts is a critical skill to learn for your health and wellness, as it will significantly reduce your suffering.**

> **Every 7 minutes you have an opportunity to change the way you feel.**

Dr. Jill Bolte Taylor, a Harvard brain neuroanatomist says the physiological lifespan of an emotion in the body and brain is **90 seconds**. She says it takes 90 seconds for the chemical components of the emotion to dissipate from the blood and the automatic response to be over. When a person has a reaction to something in their environment, there's a 90-second chemical process that happens in the body; after that, **any** remaining emotional response is the person choosing to stay in that emotional loop with their thinking. Dr. Bolte says, **if you continue to feel fear, anger, or anxiety, you need to look at the thoughts that you are thinking** as it is them that keeps re-stimulating the circuitry resulting in a prolonged physiological emotional response.

The 7-Minute Rule

It is very important during these 7-minutes when you are experiencing the emotion, NOT to take any action. It is during this time that emotions are intense, and our thinking is not at its optimal, problem-solving level. So, **as a rule, do NOT take any action during these 7 minutes and just WAIT for the emotion to pass.** Do not act on impulse, you will only regret it afterwards. So, for the first 7 minutes of your emotion WAIT. WAIT. WAIT. **We'll call this the 7-minute rule.**

If you need, put the timer on to notify yourself when the 7-minutes are up. Pausing before responding is one of the hardest things for most people to do, but very important. **After the 7-minutes is up, the logical part** of the brain will kick in and allow you to make better decisions.

Walk Through Your Emotion, Not Around It

Going through our emotions, not around them, is a concept that I find very helpful. Hard to grasp, I know, but important to understand. **Many of us try to numb, medicate, avoid, or distract ourselves from feeling our emotions.** Some use drugs, alcohol, and/or food to "numb" ourselves from feeling. Others use distraction to avoid feeling.

Some emotions feel incredibly painful, I know, and it is natural to try to do anything to not feel them. The problem is that when we try to avoid, or go around our emotions, the emotion gets bigger and grows in intensity.

The ONLY way to take charge of your anxiety and decrease its intensity is to face your emotion by pushing through it. But what does it mean to go through your emotion? Going through your emotion means "feeling it" and not being scared of it. It means dealing with it, looking it in the eye and facing it, acknowledging it and understanding it. When a sad event happens, let the sad feeling come up, feel it. Let the tears flow, feel it. And then you will notice the pain isn't so bad and the sadness doesn't have as much control over you. Whenever you feel that sad feeling come back up, let the emotion flow, don't stop it. If you feel like crying, cry.

The more time you spend trying to avoid your emotion, the bigger the problem gets. The more you go around the emotion, the more it stays there. Although it feels easier in the moment, it will only make the problem bigger and the emotion more intense. You can only avoid emotions for so long before they begin to bubble up and start to interfere in your life. **When you avoid feeling, your world becomes smaller and more restrictive**.

Unfortunately, I've lived the shrinking, more restrictive life. In order to avoid extreme anxiety, I had to stop taking my daughter places that would "trigger" her anxiety. Then one day I woke up and realized that I had put us in a corner, isolated from a lot of things that would bring her joy, like going out for dinner or traveling to see family. A much better approach would be to build skills around how to manage the anxiety in an "activated situation" and learn to work through the emotions that were coming up. When you go through the emotion, it helps you to accept what has happened so you can then either problem solve or tolerate what is happening.

> **The difference between pain and suffering is that pain comes and goes, but suffering can stay around.**

When you feel an emotion, sit and allow yourself to feel what you are feeling. Let the emotion come up, notice how it feels, and experience it. Do not judge your emotion, labeling it "good" or "bad," or saying "I shouldn't feel this way" or "I should feel that way." Just let the emotion exist.

When you just let the emotion come and go, you can process it, and get to the other side. You'll notice that you will soon begin to feel some relief from what you are feeling. The situation will no longer have as much control over you, and you will eventually be able to move on.

Mindfulness: The Key to Taking Charge of Anxiety

Mindfulness is one of my favourite concepts. It is the art of living in the NOW and accepting it 100 percent. Mindfully experiencing emotions is the opposite of trying to control your emotions. With mindfulness, you simply observe what comes up with the emotion, you notice it, and you let it go. For example, when you are scared, you notice your face is flushed, your hands are clenched or there is a lump in your throat. You notice all the experiences the emotion brings up, and you accept them unconditionally.

Mindfulness is the acceptance of the moment, being able to be in the present 100 percent and not think about the past or the future. Most of us spend the majority of our "thinking time" in either the past or the future, saying "should have," "could have," "would have," or "what if." We also get caught up in the judgement of "good" or "bad," "fair" or "unfair," and tune out of our present experience. It's almost like we "lock out" of the present moment, and "lock on" to our past.

Learning to be in the present is an acquired skill and one that needs practice.

You will notice, as you start practice your new skill, that your life will look and feel different. You might be rolling your eyes right now thinking that Mindfulness is another word for Meditation, I know I did when I first heard it. But there is no way around getting the concept of Mindfulness, it is critical. Mindfulness is a mandatory skill for good health.

Mindfulness is paying attention ONLY to what is happening right now, without judgment, without overthinking, without negating or belittling your experience, and without adding on additional thoughts and emotions.

Mindfulness is about learning how to take charge of your mind, as opposed to your mind taking charge of you. With mindfulness, you simply observe what comes up with the emotion. You notice a feeling, for example, a flushed face or a lump in your throat. You notice these "experiences" and you accept them. You do not judge them.

True acceptance is to let go of the outcome. Let go of fighting reality or wishing for something different. Facts and emotions are what they are, we cannot change them.

The act of letting go of trying to control the future, will decrease your anxiety. **The future is out of control to us. The future is uncertain**.

Practice living in the NOW—it's a beautiful place!

CHAPTER 5

CULTIVATING AN ANTI-ANXIETY MINDSET

Learning how to stop "adding on" to your original emotion is an essential skill that must be learned and fine-tuned. Without knowing it, we add on many extra thoughts and emotions to our original emotions. All the "rehearsing" of events, over and over again in our heads, only escalates the problem and keeps the "story" alive.

> There are two types of emotions:
> "Original" and "Added."

An **original emotion**, as discussed previously, is a basic emotion that comes on **immediately** to a **specific event**. You **don't have to think about it**, it comes on **automatically** and **strong**. It is the automatic reaction, or the **direct consequence** to an event. For example, you "feel happy" that your friend sent you flowers, or you "feel sad" that your friend forgot your birthday. It is a response to something internal or external.

As a reminder, the "original emotions" are:

1. Anger

2. Happiness/Joy

3. Love

4. Fear/Anxiety

5. Sadness

6. Guilt

7. Shame

An **"added emotion,"** on the other hand, is an **emotional reaction to your "Original Emotion."** It is feeling something about your initial emotion. "Added Emotions" are built over time, they don't start automatically.

They are **secondary in nature** and **take time to build in intensity. These emotions involve thinking** and **occur after a bit of time has passed.** They are feelings you ATTACH to your original emotion, like "feeling suspicious," "feeling disappointed," "feeling upset," or "feeling jealous."

Remember, original emotions only last 7 minutes (or less), try to just sit through the uncomfortable feeling, it will pass. And avoid adding on additional thoughts and emotions, once they start, it is hard to stop the spiral.

If you notice that you have already started layering your thoughts and emotions, it is important to start unravelling them to get back to the Original Emotion. It is the Original Emotion that must be addressed BEFORE you can get unstuck and free yourself from the struggles of anxiety.

> You must deal with the "added" emotions first before you can get to the original emotion. It's like "peeling back the layers of the onion" to get to the original emotion.

Anger is often a powerful added emotion. Anger often masks the original, more painful emotions such as "sadness" and "fear." Added emotions do not provide us with very much useful information, and they often **hide** or **distract** us from what is really going on with the original emotion.

"Added emotions" are things like:

- Anger
- Worry
- Apathy
- Anxiety
- Numbness
- Annoyance
- Irritability
- Frustration
- Nervousness
- Disappointment
- Loneliness
- Jealousy
- Upset

STOP, LOOK & LISTEN Technique

The STOP, LOOK & LISTEN Technique is a good, quick tool to snap you out of acting impulsively. The goal is to apply the STOP, LOOK & LISTEN Technique BEFORE too much damage is done from operating out of "too much emotion" and impulse, like breaking off a relationship or quitting a job when you have a disagreement.

Have you ever been in the middle of a fight with your partner and then say, "that's it, I want a divorce?" Or "if you don't want to listen to me, then I don't want to be your friend anymore."

The other day my friend was in a heated disagreement with her new boyfriend and all of a sudden, she said to him, "you know what, do me a favor and stay away from me." Her words were like "hot air," they were not what she really wanted, but she was really mad and would have said anything to hurt him in that moment. The truth of the matter was she was feeling very upset, sad and disappointed. The anger just took over and she acted on impulse.

Having applied the STOP, LOOK, LISTEN technique would have helped her more effectively communicate what she was feeling. The two of them could have then used their conflict resolution skills and problem solved what was really going on between the two of them.

This type of situation, where people say things to each other in the "heat of the moment," happens often in our everyday lives and causes tremendous stress and anxiety.

We want to avoid this "explosive" point and STOP the escalation BEFORE it happens. Use the technique almost like you're "putting a plug in it" or "zipping your mouth" to STOP the momentum and take a break. So as soon as you start to feel stressed, overwhelmed, panicky, angry, anxious, or out of control, apply the **Stop, Look and Listen technique**.

STOP what you're doing IMMEDIATELY. Take a physical step back, even go to the next room or walk away. Take a good look around and observe what just happened. Ask yourself "what is really going on?" Look at both sides of the situation, and then proceed to resolve the issue ONLY when you are calmed down and are in a more Balanced Mindset.

Stopping what you're doing is the hardest part. Once we are in the "fight" and have momentum, it is very difficult to stop. So, avoid getting "too hot" because if you keep going, it is very likely that too much damage will be done and you'll find yourself past the point of no return.

STOP, LOOK & LISTEN STEPS

STOP
Stop what you are doing immediately, take a step back from the situation, even go to a different room.

LOOK
Look around and observe what is going on inside and outside yourself.

LISTEN
Listen to what has been said, often we don't "hear" what the other person is saying.

PROCEED
Make appropriate adjustments in your thinking and actions and then move forward. Sometimes it's better to "talk the next day" or "talk in an hour" when you're not so emotionally charged.

Three Different Mindsets

There are three different mindsets or ways of thinking. These are the Impulsive, Rational and Balanced Mindsets. Using these "mindset" reference points is a good way to understand and hold yourself accountable to acting out of a healthy, balanced place, as opposed to coming from a place of TOO MUCH emotion or TOO MANY facts. Balanced Mind combines the "best of both worlds" and is the place you want to focus being most of the time. It's acting in a healthy, balanced way, combining emotions and facts, logic and intuition.

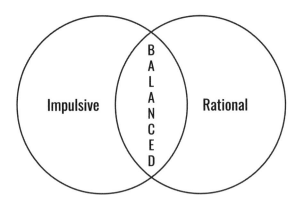

The **rational mindset** is the "thinking" brain where they make decisions based 100 percent on facts. Decisions are made ONLY based on fact, logic, and statistics. There is no regard for emotions or empathy at all. The problem with operating this way is the person does not factor emotions into their decision making. This leaves them cut off from people feelings, so at times it makes interpersonal relations difficult when they only operate on facts. It also exposes them to making poor decisions as they're not looking at the "whole picture" when they only look at facts.

The **impulsive mindset** is the "feeling" brain where the person acts 100 percent out of emotion, impulse and "gut feeling." No attention is given to facts, logic or reason. There is no logic or long-term thinking factor in their decision-making process, it is all based on a feeling. It's all emotion, intuition, gut feeling, and impulse. Acting emotionally can be beneficial at times, but it can also be damaging because they act impulsively, in the heat of the moment with no proof, reason or rationality. For example, if someone's having a bad day, they might quit work or break up with their partner, because that's how they felt that day.

The **balanced mindset** is the combination of both the rational and impulsive. **The person synergizes information using logic and emotion, and formulates an opinion based on all information**. The Balanced Mind is the best way to operate as it considers all information. The balanced individual can think, act and solve problems with a combination of intuition AND facts. They are neither too emotional nor too logical.

It is a good idea to strive to be in the balanced mindset the majority of the time acting with intention, facts, and confidence.

CHAPTER 6

MOVING FORWARD AND TAKING ACTION

O ur minds are full of thoughts all day long. Sometimes we have good thoughts, sometimes we have not so good thoughts. **Thoughts are each person's interpretation of the situation.** The mind is constantly trying to make sense of the world, forming judgements and opinions about every situation. Although we all start out with accurate assumptions, the thought process can be biased and cause us to reach the wrong conclusion. Therefore, it is important to question our thoughts.

Our thoughts are influenced by our core belief system. Our opinions are shaped from things we have seen and heard in the past and those opinions affect what we see. **The problem is our thoughts are not always necessarily true.** Without even realizing it, we are interpreting and giving our "own" meaning to everything that is happening around us. We might decide when something is pleasant or unpleasant, good or bad, safe or dangerous based on the past. **Sometimes our thoughts even "blow things out of proportion" and make the situation worse.**

Our own thoughts and beliefs often cause us more anxiety than the actual emotion itself. And sometimes our beliefs are faulty or inaccurate. **In order to get to the facts, it's important to question your thoughts and NOT always believe everything that you think.**

The goal of this chapter is to get your **mind and body into a state where you can think more clearly,** stay in the moment and problem solve. This is the time when we figure things out.

A critical concept in this **thinking stage** is to focus on the NOW. This means avoid putting your thinking energy in the future and what "could" happen. Many of us fear the future. And it's this fear of the future that causes us anxiety. **The future however is out of control to us.** The future is uncertain.

Worry is NOT based on facts.
Worry is the FEAR of the future.

Be Aware of Your Own Judgemental Words

Judging is a quick way of stating how you "feel" about a situation. It is taking the facts about a situation and adding your own personal experiences, values and opinions to make an objective truth.

Although judgments can be helpful in organizing our experiences into categories, they are spontaneous and often inaccurate interpretations of reality. Judgements are NOT the facts. Judgements come from the mind of the observer; they are NOT what is really going on. Describing the judgement, the view from the person, is not effective communication and does not get you very far. Judgements come in the form of words like should, shouldn't, good, bad, right, wrong, fair, unfair, deserve, don't deserve, terrible, and failure.

Judgements influence our thinking and behavior, affecting the outcome of a situation. Judgements are often made towards other people and things, but the most damaging judgements are what we make towards ourselves.

Judgemental words include any of the following:

- Right, wrong
- Good, bad
- Fair, unfair
- Should, shouldn't
- Deserve, don't deserve
- Dumb, clever
- Stupid, lazy
- Wonderful, horrible
- Perfect, terrible
- Never

The goal is to lead a non-judgemental life and separate your opinion from the facts. It is a good idea to concentrate on stating what the facts are as opposed to reporting your opinion.

Here are some clues that you might be fighting reality:

- Feeling bitter or resentful

- Thinking your life should not be this way

- Feeling regularly unhappy or frustrated with life

- Thinking that if "something" changed, you would be happy

- Trying to force other people to change their behaviors

Check Your Proportions

At times when we are feeling anxious, **we blow things out of proportion**. We imagine the **worst possible outcome of an action or an event**. For example, if you have one bad night sleep, you will never be able to sleep again. You have one fight with your spouse, and you are getting a divorce.

Unfortunately, when we "blow things out of proportion" or "catastrophize" things, we only make our anxiety worse. We fill our minds with emotions and thoughts that take time and energy away from the reality of the situation and add a great deal of unnecessary stress.

Learn to Tolerate Uncertainty

Another very important part of moving forward is learning to tolerate uncertainty. Whenever I get that uncomfortable feeling, I need to remind myself to just sit through it, that it is going to be okay. I literally have to coach myself through the uncomfortable feeling of "anxiety" and "not knowing" and tell myself that it will feel better tomorrow. If you're having a tough time, this is a great time to practice your calming exercises to activate your parasympathetic nervous system. Focus on doing calming exercises for your 6 senses. Have a warm bath, hug your pet, dance around the house, get a pedicure, or put on a heated blanket.

Although dealing with uncertainty is an unavoidable part of life, anxious people have a very hard time NOT knowing what's going to happen. The uncertainty of not knowing what is going to happen, causes a lot of stress.

Anxious people will often try to plan
and prepare for everything as a way of
avoiding or eliminating uncertainty.

My friend who suffers from a lot of anxiety would call me around 10 times before our dinner date to make sure that I was going to be there and not leave her sitting alone. At first, I didn't understand why she had to call me so many times. But eventually I realized that it was her way of controlling the situation. Her way of dealing with the uncertainty of not knowing and protect herself from the pain and disappointment of sitting there alone.

Anxious people might do things like ask a lot of questions, make lists, double check, procrastinate, avoid or seek excessive reassurance. Although these behaviours help people cope in the moment, they consume a lot of time and energy and are unproductive in helping you overcome anxiety.

It is important to accept that we cannot
control everything and must increase our
ability to tolerate uncertainty and change.

By becoming more tolerant of uncertainty and change, you will realize that you can deal with things even when they do not go as expected.

Accepting the situation is truly accepting the present moment 100 percent. It is not about changing the present or changing the past, it is accepting the situation for what it is. It is important to understand that you do NOT have to agree with the problem, like it, or approve of it, but it's important to accept the problem for what it is.

When we do not accept reality, we fight against it, **wishing things were different** or **fixating on how they "should" or "could" be**.

> **The more we fight AGAINST pain or reality, the more likely we are to experience negative emotions such as anger and sadness.**

We all have pain in our lives from time to time. Pain is seen as a distressing, objective feeling that we all have. **It is how we "react" to the pain that determines our "suffering."**

Suffering on the other hand, is a choice. **Suffering is a subjective, emotion-driven experience of how pain affects you.** Suffering is NOT accepting the here and now.

The more we complain and push AGAINST acceptance, the more the suffering will increase. On the other
hand, **once we accept the situation, we can let go of
the suffering and move on. Only then can we change**.

For example, you do not have to like your dimples,
but they are there, and you can't change that. But if you
accept and love them for what they are, you will feel a
lot better about yourself.

> PAIN - ACCEPTANCE = SUFFERING
>
> or
>
> PAIN + ACCEPTANCE = CHANGE

Make a Commitment

Another part of moving forward is making a commitment. With **non-committal thinking**, you'll find
yourself saying "I'll try" or "I'll do my best." This type of
thinking is guaranteed to not move you forward. When
you say the words "I'll try" or "I'll do my best," they are
empty words with very little intention of ever doing
what you say you are going to do.

In order to move forward and change your life, you must commit to **taking action**. You don't need to do huge action steps, but do make a commitment, even to do something very small, so you can begin to move forward. Commit 100 percent and follow through.

Avoid using the words "I'll try" or "I'll do my best."

Take Action and Solve Your Problem

This is the step where you synthesize all the information you have gathered and make a final resolve. To problem solve, you need to identify your current problem or stressor. Then ask yourself how you can solve the problem. Allow yourself time to think, get the facts, and take yourself seriously. Keep it neutral and avoid judging or criticizing yourself.

You've gathered all the information, accepted where things are at, and now you're at the final decision-making time. I've picked two problem-solving exercises to help you work through and solve your problems.

The first one involves looking at the pros and cons of doing something, and then the pros and cons of not doing something. I like to use this example because it helps you to identify all aspects of the problem, shedding light on the situation and your "feelings" about the situation. The second exercise involves changing how you think, feel and react to the situation.

Four Squares Exercise

IDENTIFY THE ISSUE/PROBLEM

Pros of Doing	Cons of Doing
Pros of Not Doing	**Cons of Not Doing**

Here's an example of the four squares exercise in action:

GOING ON AN AIRPLANE

Pros of Doing	Cons of Doing
• I'll get to visit with family	• It's expensive
• I'll get to have a vacation	• I'll feel anxious
• I'll get to see new things	• I'll have difficulty sleeping
• I'll get to sit in the sun	• I'll have to face my fear of flying
• I'll get to go to the beach	• It'll be a change in my routine
• I'll get to relax at the pool	

Pros of Not Doing	Cons of Not Doing
• I don't have to push myself	• I'll stay stuck
• I don't have to face my fears	• I'll miss out on the fun
• I don't have to spend money	• I'll feel isolated from my loved ones
• I get to stay safe	• I'll feel depressed and lonely
• My routine stays unchanged	• I'll miss out on seeing family

Paths to Problem Solving

There are five different paths to solving a problem:

Solve the Problem

This is where you change the situation. You do something about the problem.

The person can "solve the problem" of feeling lonely by joining a social group like a hiking club, book club, or salsa dance class to meet new people with similar interests.

Change How You "Feel" About the Problem

This is where you change how you "feel" about the situation.

The person can decide NOT to change the situation, but rather how they "feel" about the situation. For example, they can choose to "feel better" about being an introvert, reassuring themselves that it's okay to do things on their own. It does not mean something is wrong with them or that they are unlikable.

Tolerate the Problem

This is where you decide to "accept" the situation and change your opinion of the problem.

The person can choose to "accept the situation" rather than trying to solve being lonely or change the way they "feel" about being lonely. For example, they can learn to "tolerate" not having many friends and "accept" that being alone is part of life. They have a busy work life and family life that make it hard to have lots of friends.

Decide To Let It Go

This is where you decide to "let go of the problem," move on and stop struggling.

The person can "make a decision" to let the problem go, stop the struggling, and move on. For example, they can decide that they don't need more friends, they are happy the way they are.

Don't Change

This is where you decide to do nothing. The problem and the struggles both remain.

The person can choose not to do anything about the problem and stay the same.

Avoid Avoiding

It's important to avoid avoiding. The typical rule is, **the more we avoid, the bigger the problem gets.** For example, if you are fearful of flying, you will not go on a plane. But if you do not challenge your problem, you will never fly. The better approach would be able to acknowledge that you are fearful of flying, and then do something about it, like get on a short flight, even if it is for a half an hour.

The strategy is to **figure out what level of problem solving you feel is challenging enough and then push that level** by building a plan around how you are going to conquer or master your fear. Start slowly and take forward-moving action steps, one at a time until eventually you can get on the plane.

It is a good idea to check in to see if you have any limiting beliefs. You just might discover a belief that is keeping you stuck.

Create Your Action Plan

Setting your action plan involves setting goals, defining objectives, determining action steps, and reflecting back. I find the best exercise for goal setting and creating an action plan is the Wheel of Balance Exercise.

Life is like a wheel and every aspect of our life is a spoke in that wheel. When properly balanced, the wheel functions well. But, if one spoke breaks or bends, it affects the entire wheel. The same analogy applies to life. If one area of our life is challenging or bears too much weight, our whole "wheel" becomes out of balance and we can feel stressed, overwhelmed, unhealthy, or unhappy.

Like a wheel, we operate as a system where each area of importance in your life works in relation to everything else. Each spoke depends on the other spokes so the wheel can function properly. Shifting attention to a more balanced approach takes the "pressure off" certain areas of your life that are more challenging. If you can create success in other areas of your life, you will feel better about yourself overall.

When goal setting, it is important to create a plan where the goals are specific, manageable, and measurable. We want to avoid getting overwhelmed with setting huge goals and feeling upset for not accomplishing them. We also want to avoid getting overwhelmed with the number of spokes/areas to focus on. This exercise is about small steps. You can always go back and do this exercise a second or third time.

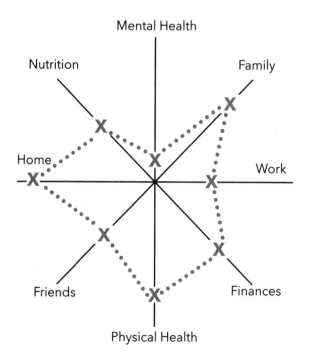

1) **Label each spoke as an area that is important to YOU** (i.e., work, career, health, finances, family, kids, mental health, friends, relationship, body weight). Add more lines if needed. There is no right or wrong answer. It is what is important to you.

2) **Indicate where on the "feel" scale you are on each spoke with a small line or X.** Quantify from 0–10 along the line from the middle axis point until the end of the line. 0 as not so good, to 10 being excellent. Do this for each spoke. When completed, draw a line connecting the X's.

3) **Now take a step back and reflect.** Look at how your wheel looks. Is it a wheel that looks like it would function well?

4) **Now take a different color pen and indicate where you "want" to be on each spoke.** Yes, you can be at the 10 for each spoke if you want. Now draw a line connecting those newly marked areas.

5) **List a goal statement for each spoke.** Try not to create too big of a goal that would be too overwhelming to accomplish. Keep it specific and measurable. Even the act of writing down a goal is a huge accomplishment.

Writing down a goal is 50 percent of the work in getting there.

6) **Write down 1–3 action steps for each goal.** Baby action steps are fantastic.

Words of Encouragement

Goal setting and creating an action plan takes time and effort. Try not to get overwhelmed by the big goal or the number of spokes.

Focus on taking small action steps for each spoke and soon you'll notice that you have accomplished more than you thought. Remember to be compassionate with yourself and act in a gentle, supportive, and understanding way.

You CAN do it!

CONCLUSION

A major reason that many of us suffer from anxiety today is because we have "felt unheard" or "dismissed" in our lives. We were told that we "weren't good enough" or that we "shouldn't feel a certain way." This negative environment taught us not to trust ourselves, and not to trust our emotions. As a result, we have a lot of self-doubt and anxiety.

On top of that, many of us project fears from the past into the future. Very rarely do we go into a situation without the "baggage" and "opinions" that we have carried from past experiences.

You have now learned several new and important self-help skills and techniques that can help you stop YOUR negative cycles in their tracks and create NEW, positive results. I know these techniques worked very well for me and the people I've taught, and now they can work for you too.

The present is full of wonderful new opportunities. Allow yourself to live and experience new things. Trying to paint over an old painting never turns out very well. Try treating every new experience as a "blank canvas" and give yourself the opportunity to create something beautiful.

By working hard and being open to change, we can become unstuck from the past.

We CAN take control of our mind. We CAN stop the divergent, repetitive, and unhealthy thoughts from reoccurring. We CAN create a new present with less anxiety.

It's time to treat yourself with respect.

It's time to believe in yourself.

It's time to change your present.

It's time to change your future.

You are worth it.

You deserve to live your best life.

ANXIETY MANAGEMENT EXERCISES

Starting a Conversation

If your anxiety could talk, what would it say?

_____

_____

_____

_____

Now, if you could talk back to your anxiety, what would you say?

_____

_____

_____

_____

Forward Thinking

If your life was free of anxiety, what would it look like?

_____

_____

_____

_____

How would you feel? What would be different from now?

_____

_____

_____

_____

Daily Survival Kit

Here's how to create a daily anxiety survival kit to help you address your anxiety right when it happens. The key is activating your six senses to help you contextualize your feelings and re-center. Feel free to carry this kit around with you and use these techniques several times a day, whenever you're feeling anxious.

- **Taste:** Chew strongly flavored gum or sour gummies.

- **Sight:** Look at an image that you love, a photo that brings you "back" to a special place.

- **Smell:** Put on lip balm, essential oil, suntan lotion, or favorite lotion or body wash.

- **Touch:** Take a hot shower or bath, get a body massage, or manicure or pedicure.

- **Hearing:** Put on your favorite music playlist, sounds of the ocean, or a favorite song.

- **Proprioception:** Ride on a tire swing, apply a weighted blanket, vest or jacket for deep pressure, or use a body massager in thumping mode.

What are some other things you can use to activate your senses? Brainstorm some ways that will work well for you:

Sight

1. _____

2. _____

3. _____

Taste

1. _____

2. _____

3. _____

Smell

1. _____

2. _____

3. _____

Hearing

1. _____

2. _____

3. _____

Touch

1. _____

2. _____

3. _____

Proprioception

1. _____

2. _____

3. _____

Prepare Your Emergency Plan

This plan is to be used when your anxiety levels are particularly high, to shock your body and mind into a different state.

Temperature change: Sudden temperature change quickly "cools" the body and mind down. Do it long enough that it will make a difference. For example, take a freezing cold shower, splash cold water on your face 10 times or put your head under freezing cold tap water. If you have ice, hold an ice cube in your hand for 30 seconds to 1 minute (or for as long as you can handle it, but do not hurt yourself).

Intense exercise: Intense exercise shocks the body by increasing oxygen in the body and decreasing your stress level quickly. Sprint to the end of the block, do burpees or jumping jacks until exhaustion. Run up a hill.

What are 5–10 things can you do to shock your body quickly (and safely) and effectively?

1) _____

2) _____

3) _____

4) _____

5) _____

6) _____

7) _____

8) _____

9) _____

10) _____

Decode Your Emotions

There is an old expression: "You can't argue with an emotion." This is because our emotions are there for a reason. Your emotions give you valuable information;

they are the key to understanding what is happening inside of you. Emotional regulation is the ability to effectively manage and respond to an emotional experience. People unconsciously use emotion regulation strategies to cope with difficult situations that come up all the time throughout the day. Some of us have a natural ability to regulate our emotions, while others of us must learn how to manage these emotions in a healthy way.

Today I felt . . .

_____

_____

_____

_____

_____

Question Your Thoughts

Our own "added-on" thoughts and beliefs often cause more anxiety and suffering than needed. Stop, think and question your thoughts. Remember we want to problem solve the initial emotion.

Event

_____

_____

_____

Initial Thought

_____

_____

Added on Thoughts

_____

_____

_____

Original Emotion

_____

_____

_____

Added on Emotions

_____

_____

_____

Practice Using Balanced Mindset

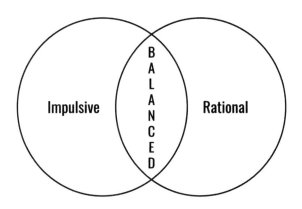

Impulsive Mindset: We act impulsively out of emotions and feelings only.

Rational Mindset: We act rationally out of logic and facts only.

Balanced Mindset: We synthesize facts AND emotions and act wisely, in a healthy way.

Today I acted this way:

_____

_____

My balanced mind would have acted:

_____

_____

_____

Today I acted this way:

_____

_____

My balanced mind would have acted:

_____

_____

_____

Today I acted this way:

_____

_____

My balanced mind would have acted:

_____

_____

_____

Four Squares: Pros and Cons Problem Solving

IDENTIFY THE ISSUE/PROBLEM

Pros of Doing	Cons of Doing
Pros of Not Doing	Cons of Not Doing

Practice Effective Problem-Solving

1) Identify the problem.

2) Change the situation.

3) Change the emotional reaction.

4) Accept and tolerate the problem.

5) Make a decision to let the problem go.

6) Do not change your mind.

What is your current problem? Be specific.

_____

_____

How can you change the situation? What action can you take to make it better?

_____

_____

_____

How can you change how you "feel" about the situation or the problem?

_____

_____

_____

_____

How can you better accept and tolerate the problem?

_____

_____

_____

_____

I will let the problem go.

_____

_____

_____

I won't change.

_____

_____

Re-Working Your Negative Beliefs

For example: I used to believe that <u>everyone thought</u> <u>I was stupid so I wouldn't put my hand up in class or talk</u> <u>to anybody which made me feel isolated.</u>

Now I believe that <u>everybody has strengths and weak-</u> <u>nesses, and the important thing is to try. The only way to</u> <u>move forward in life is to try. If you make a mistake, see it</u> <u>as a stepping-stone, rather than a stumbling block.</u>

I used to believe . . .

_____

_____

_____

Now I believe . . .

_____

_____

_____

I used to believe . . .

_____

_____

_____

Now I believe . . .

_____

_____

_____

Brain Training: Celebrate the Small Things

Changing your thinking takes practice, begin by acknowledging the little bits of enjoyment or success you experience every day. **Every day, acknowledge 5–10 good things that happened**, they can be the smallest little things, like "I got out of bed," or "I washed my face."

For example, today I:

1. Got a hug and kiss from my puppy.

2. Bought my favorite lip gloss.

3. Said "hi" to my neighbour.

4. Talked to my sister on the phone.

5. Used my favorite bodywash that smelled like summer.

6. Went for a long walk with my dog.

7. Made a nice dinner for myself.

8. Sat in the sun for 15 minutes to drink my favorite tea and relax.

Today I . . .

1. _____

2. _____

3. _____

4. _____

5. _____

6. _____

7. _____

8. _____

9. _____

10. _____

Building Positive Self-Talk

Self-talk is the internal dialogue that runs in your head, your inner voice. The words you say to yourself, about yourself, that others cannot hear. This talk plays a critical role in shaping how you feel about yourself. In fact, it shapes your life. It tells the brain what to believe by giving it messages and clues of your inner world, your true feelings.

To get you feeling happier and healthier, it is important to turn that self-talk into positive talk. We don't want to apply a "Band-Aid approach," we want to work on shifting your true thoughts and feelings about yourself. Letting some good feelings in, building your confidence and self-worth. A good exercise to do is to start by writing down some words or phrases that you notice yourself saying about yourself. Then come up with a "nice" list of things to say to yourself.

Write down words or comments you noticed that you said about yourself today.

1. _____

2. _____

3. _____

4. _____

5. _____

What five "nice" things, comments or good qualities can you say about yourself today? Pick something ever so small if you need, even if it's a nice eyelash!

1. _____

2. _____

3. _____

4. _____

5. _____

Body Awareness Exercise: Improving your Interoceptive Awareness

Take a self-inventory of your body and ask yourself, "Today, do I have any of the following symptoms of anxiety? Tick off the one(s) that apply to you.

- Headache
- Tight shoulders
- Stomach ache
- Sore neck
- Sore back
- Sore hips
- Sore eyes
- Sore feet
- Tired legs

Now, ask yourself if you are experiencing any of the following:

- Hungry

- Thirsty

- Tired

- Anxious

- Cold

- Hot

- Feeling disconnected from my body

Spokes of the Wheel Exercise

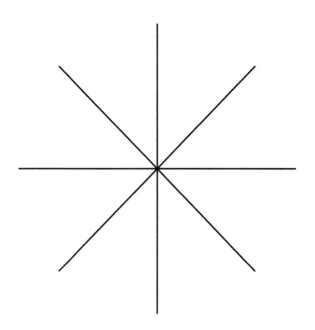

Identify your spokes:

1. _____

2. _____

3. _____

4. _____

5. _____

6. _____

7. _____

8. _____

Write a goal statement for each spoke:

1. _____

2. _____

3. _____

4. _____

5. _____

6. _____

7. _____

8. _____

Write down 1–3 action steps for each spoke goal. Then accomplish one action step at a time. It's best if the action step has a time frame to it.

Action Steps for Goal 1

1. _____

2. _____

3. _____

Action Steps for Goal 2

1. _____

2. _____

3. _____

Action Steps for Goal 3

1. _____

2. _____

3. _____

Action Steps for Goal 4

1. _____

2. _____

3. _____

Action Steps for Goal 5

1. _____
2. _____
3. _____

Action Steps for Goal 6

1. _____
2. _____
3. _____

Action Steps for Goal 7

1. _____
2. _____
3. _____

Action Steps for Goal 8

1. _____
2. _____
3. _____

ABOUT THE AUTHOR

 **Michelle Biton** is a leader and innovator in the health and wellness field. She has been inspiring women worldwide over the past 30 years through her books, newsletters and websites. Michelle is a health and wellness coach, mental health advocate and author of the best-selling book *Pregnancy Without Pounds*. Michelle is passionate about writing self-help books that empower people to change, implement healthy choices and live their best life possible.

Michelle has her master's degree in Holistic Nutrition, a bachelor's degree in Psychology and a Certificate in Applied Science Health and Fitness Studies. Michelle has a background coaching people in mental health, addictions recovery, sensory integration disorder, behavioral coaching, disordered eating and lots of anxiety.

Currently, anxiety is the number one mental health disorder in the United States, with roughly 40 million people suffering annually and growing rapidly. Sadly, only an estimated 37 percent receive professional help, largely due to affordability and accessibility issues.

It is Michelle's passion in writing this self-help book to coach and inspire many more people to push through their challenges with anxiety. To give people hope that they **can** change. To give people an understanding and the tools necessary to know **how** to change.

The Instant Anxiety Solution is an essential read for every person struggling with anxiety. The self-help skills and invaluable lessons learned will help the reader in all areas of life.

Learn more at www.michellebiton.com.

Open Journal

_____

_____

_____

_____

_____

_____

_____

_____

_____

_____

_____

_____

_____

_____

_____

_____

_____

Open Journal

_____

_____

_____

_____

_____

_____

_____

_____

_____

_____

_____

_____

_____

_____

_____

_____

_____

Open Journal

_____

_____

_____

_____

_____

_____

_____

_____

_____

_____

_____

_____

_____

_____

Open Journal

Open Journal

_____

_____

_____

_____

_____

_____

_____

_____

_____

_____

_____

_____

_____

_____

_____

_____

_____

_____

Open Journal

_____

_____

_____

_____

_____

_____

_____

_____

_____

_____

_____

_____

_____

_____

_____

_____

_____

_____

_____